Y0-BLS-685

ON WITH THE SHOW

Show Me Riddles

by Rick & Ann Walton
pictures by Susan Slattery Burke

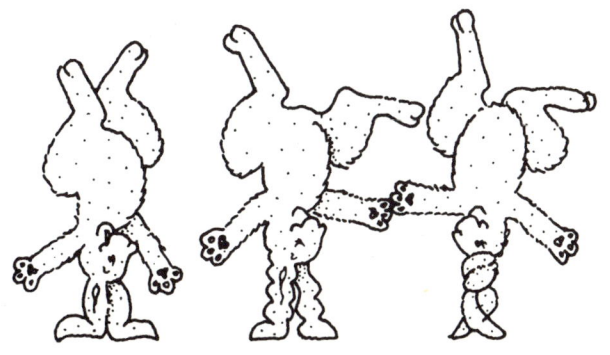

L Lerner Publications Company · Minneapolis

To MLEIV, who will show the world   —R.W. & A.W.

To my wonderful husband, Nick, who puts up with my "creative process" and loves me anyway   —S.S.B.

Copyright © 1990 by Lerner Publications Company

All rights reserved. International copyright secured. No part of this book may be reproduced in any form whatsoever without permission in writing from the publisher except for the inclusion of brief quotations in an acknowledged review.

Library of Congress Cataloging-in-Publication Data

Walton, Rick.
   On with the show: show me riddles/by Rick & Ann Walton; pictures by Susan Slattery Burke.
      p. cm.—(You must be joking)
   Summary: A collection of Show-me riddles, e.g. "Show me a pencil that itches... And I'll show you scratch paper."
   ISBN 0-8225-2327-2 (lib. bdg.)
   1. Riddles, Juvenile. 2. Wit and humor, Juvenile. [1. Riddles.]
I. Walton, Ann, 1963-   . II. Burke, Susan Slattery, ill.
III. Title. IV. Series.
PN6371.5.W36   1990
818'.5402—dc20   89-36631
                                                           CIP
                                                            AC

Manufactured in the United States of America

1 2 3 4 5 6 7 8 9 10   99 98 97 96 95 94 93 92 91 90

Show me a herd of cows who play the trombone...
And I'll show you longhorn cattle.

Show me a cowboy
on a giraffe...
And I'll show you
someone who is
riding high.

Show me a miner who digs with an elephant
   tusk…
And I'll show you a tooth pick.

Show me Julius Caesar's sow…
And I'll show you pig latin.

Show me a pig in a Porsche…
And I'll show you a road hog.

Show me a flooded parking lot…
And I'll show you a carpool.

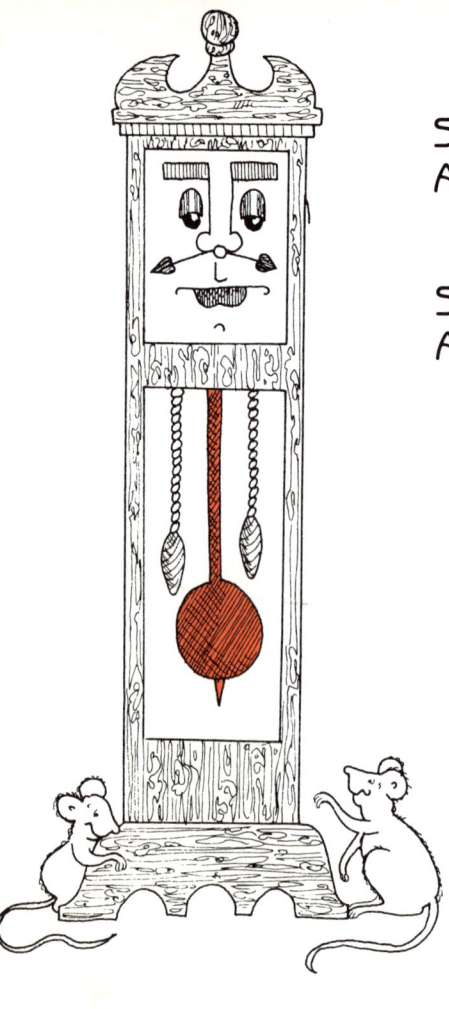

Show me a freeway collision...
And I'll show you a smash hit.

Show me a tugboat used by the navy...
And I'll show you a tug-o'-war.

Show me a grandfather clock...
And I'll show you an old-timer.

Show me a hiker who's careless with
    matches...
And I'll show you a trailblazer.

Show me a girl who rides sunbeams...
And I'll show you a girl who travels
    light.

Show me a mamma flea...
And I'll show you a woman who's
    afraid that her children are going
    to the dogs.

Show me ants wearing elevator shoes…
And I'll show you tolerance.

Show me spiders living in your shoes…
And I'll show you webbed feet.

Show me a flaming arrow…
And I'll show you a fire fly.

Show me insects in Italy…
And I'll show you Rome-ants.

Show me a puppy who likes to go for a ride…
And I'll show you a car-pet.

Show me a sad garbage collector…
And I'll show you someone who is down in the dumps.

Show me a cat who throws his garbage anywhere…
And I'll show you kitty litter.

Show me a tornado in a pool hall…
And I'll show you a whirlpool.

Show me day break…
And I'll show you the crack of dawn.

Show me a rained-out picnic…
And I'll show you a wet blanket.

Show me a houseboat with a hole in the
   hull…
And I'll show you the kitchen sink.

Show me a gangster in the shower...
And I'll show you a crook who has come clean.

Show me a track star who works out with her husband…
And I'll show you a running mate.

Show me a champion bowler…
And I'll show you someone who knows how to get the ball rolling.

Show me a duck hunter at a basketball game…
And I'll show you a foul shot.

Show me a track meet for athletic buildings…
And I'll show you a bank vault.

Show me a house that has grown legs and started racing off down the street...
And I'll show you a home run.

Show me a predatory bird who is
    afraid of the dark…
And I'll show you a chicken hawk.

Show me a turkey on the telephone…
And I'll show you a bird call.

Show me a boy who only goes
    roller skating when he
    doesn't have to pay…
And I'll show you a cheap skate.

Show me a sparrow in a tornado…
And I'll show you a whirlybird.

Show me a sad robin…
And I'll show you a blue bird.

Show me an Ozark mountain goat…
And I'll show you a hill billy.

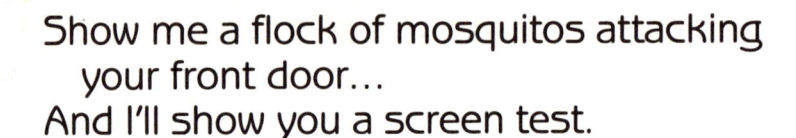

Show me a flock of mosquitos attacking
   your front door...
And I'll show you a screen test.

Show me a girl who's allergic to the
   alphabet...
And I'll show you B-hives.

Show me a bumblebee
   ringing your doorbell...
And I'll show you a hum-dinger.

Show me a fireworks
   show…
And I'll show you
   the high lights.

Show me a messy pirate drinking
   grape juice…
And I'll show you Bluebeard.

Show me a giant…
And I'll show you
   someone to look up to.

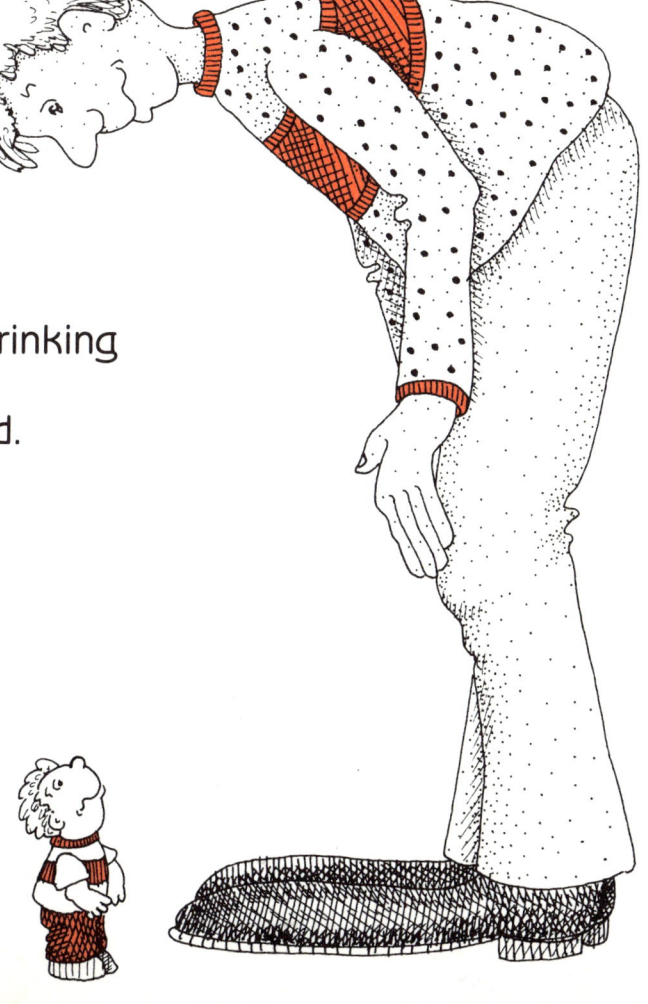

Show me a sneezing dragon...
And I'll show you a blowtorch.

Show me a bald giant…
And I'll show you a big wig.

Show me King Kong coming out of a cannon…
And I'll show you a big shot.

Show me King Kong playing cards with the Jolly Green Giant…
And I'll show you a big deal.

Show me King Kong's unicycle…
And I'll show you a big wheel.

Show me Dracula's boat…
And I'll show you a blood vessel.

Show me Dracula's safety deposit box…
And I'll show you a blood bank.

Show me the skeleton of a genie…
And I'll show you a wishbone.

Show me a banquet for skeletons…
And I'll show you spare ribs.

Show me a mystery novel…
And I'll show you a bookcase.

Show me a pencil that itches…
And I'll show you scratch paper.

Show me a small child with
 a crayon…
And I'll show you someone
 who sees the handwriting
 on the wall.

Show me an orchestra conductor...
And I'll show you someone who has to face the music.

Show me a breeze whistling through the trees...
And I'll show you a woodwind.

Show me a traveling violinist...
And I'll show you someone who likes to fiddle around.

Show me a percussionist covered
   with glue...
And I'll show you a drum stick.

Show me the person who sets
   up the sound equipment for a
   rock group...
And I'll show you a band aid.

Show me a lamb playing a tuba...
And I'll show you a bighorn sheep.

Show me a school gym…
And I'll show you a ballroom.

Show me a candy man…
And I'll show you a sweetheart.

Show me a boxing banana…
And I'll show you fruit punch.

Show me a party for movie actors and
    prison inmates…
And I'll show you the Stars and Stripes.

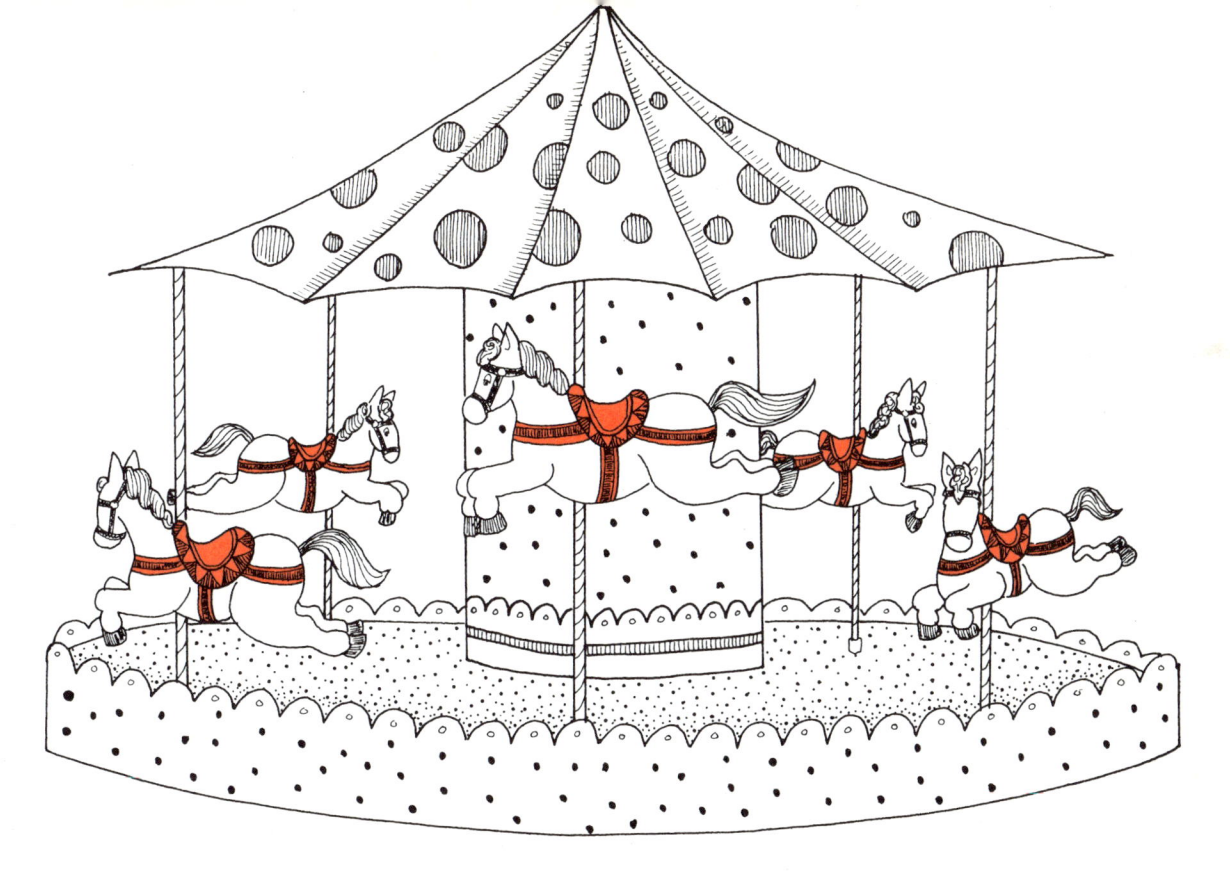

Show me a merry-go-round... And I'll show you a round trip.

Show me a surfer who's proud of his hair...
And I'll show you a beachcomber.

Show me a rabbit trainer...
And I'll show you someone who can make his hare stand on end.

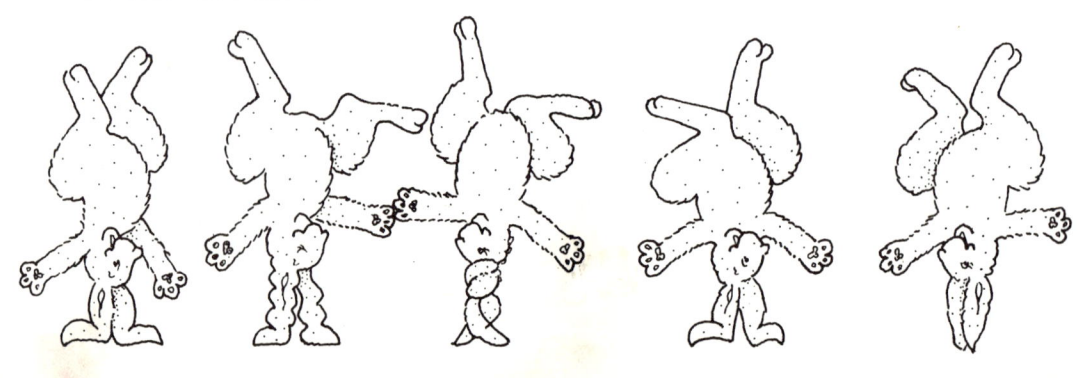

Show me a zookeeper who doesn't give the
     monkeys all the bananas she promises…
And I'll show you a cheetah.

Show me a boss who sees everything her
     employees do…
And I'll show you supervision.

Show me a store owned by primates…
And I'll show you monkey business.

Show me a boy who's tired of summer…
And I'll show you a boy who's ready for a fall.

Show me a sundial in December…
And I'll show you wintertime.

Show me a girl kissing an ice cube…
And I'll show you a lip stick.

Show me a tornado in a small town…
And I'll show you a house fly.

Show me a battle between two groups of Eskimos...
And I'll show you a cold war.

ABOUT THE AUTHORS

Rick and Ann Walton love to read, travel, play guitar, study foreign languages, and write for children. Rick also collects books and writes music while Ann knits and does origami. They live in Provo, Utah, where Ann is a computer programmer and Rick is practicing to be a moose wrestler. They have two incredible children.

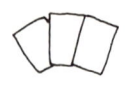

ABOUT THE ARTIST

Susan Slattery Burke loves to illustrate fun-loving characters, especially animals. To her, each of them has a personality all their own. Her satisfaction comes when the characters come to life for the reader. Susan lives in Minneapolis, Minnesota, with her husband, her dog, and her cat. She is a graduate of the University of Minnesota. Susan enjoys sculpting, travel, illustrating, entertaining, and being outdoors.

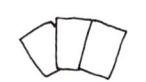

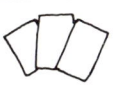

You Must Be Joking

Help Wanted:
  Riddles about Jobs

Here's to Ewe:
  Riddles about Sheep

On with the Show:
  Show Me Riddles

Out on a Limb:
  Riddles about Trees and Plants

Weather or Not:
  Riddles for Rain and Shine

What's Gnu?
  Riddles from the Zoo

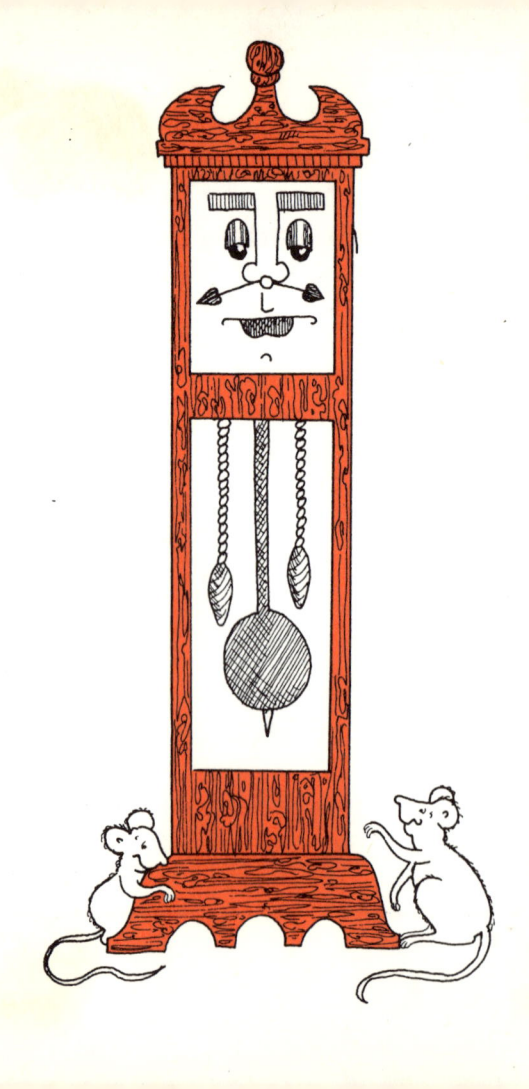

818 Walton, Rick
WAL
     On with the show

$7.95   43724

DATE			

© THE BAKER & TAYLOR CO.